MARY FRANK SCHOOL LIBRARY

T 1423

Mary Frank Library
P-H-M School Corporation
Mishawaka, Indiana

S0-CPE-893

523
Ham   Hamer, Martyn

           The night sky

OEMCO

AN
EASY-READ
FACT
BOOK

The Night Sky

Martyn Hamer

Mary Frank Library
P-H-M School Corporation
Mishawaka, Indiana

Franklin Watts
London   New York   Toronto   Sydney

© 1983 Franklin Watts Ltd

First published in Great Britain
   1983 by
Franklin Watts Ltd
12a Golden Square
London W1

First published in the USA by
Franklin Watts Inc.
387 Park Avenue South
New York
N.Y. 10016

UK ISBN: 0 86313 018 6
US ISBN: 0-531-04619-2
Library of Congress Catalog Card
   Number: 82-62986

Printed in Great Britain by
   Cambus Litho, East Kilbride

Designed and produced by
David Jefferis

Illustrated by
Russell Barnett
Hayward Art Group
Hayward and Martin
Michael Roffe

Photographs supplied by
NASA
Space Frontiers Ltd

Technical consultant
Iain Nicholson BSc, FRAS

The Night Sky

Contents

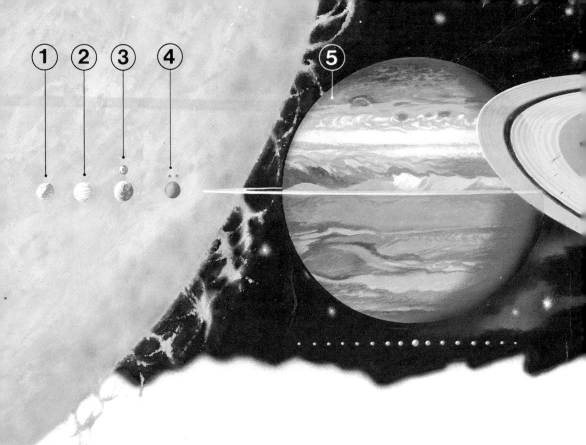

The Earth in space

The Earth is one of nine planets that move around the Sun. All but two planets have moons which move around them. The Sun and its "family" of planets, moons and other space debris is called the Solar System.

▷ The Sun is just one star in a spiral cluster of 100 billion stars called the Milky Way galaxy. There are millions of other galaxies in space.

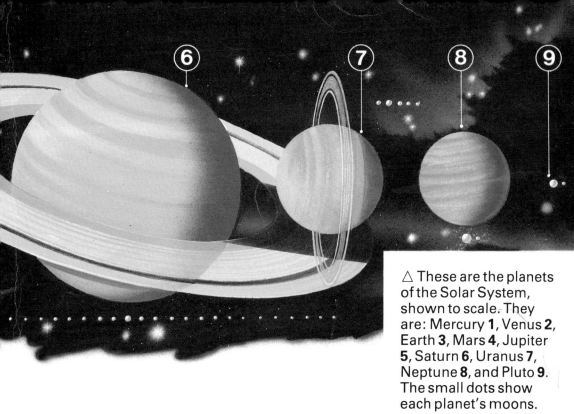

△ These are the planets of the Solar System, shown to scale. They are: Mercury **1**, Venus **2**, Earth **3**, Mars **4**, Jupiter **5**, Saturn **6**, Uranus **7**, Neptune **8**, and Pluto **9**. The small dots show each planet's moons.

Our neighbor, the Moon

Our nearest neighbor in space is the Moon. It is only 239,000 miles (384,000 km) away – just a stone's throw compared to the immense size of the Universe.

The Moon is not a planet, but a natural satellite of the Earth. As our world orbits the Sun, so the Moon orbits the Earth. It takes 27 days 8 hours to complete one orbit.

As the Moon moves around the Earth, it appears to change shape. These changes, or phases, happen because the Moon has no light of its own. Its light is just reflected sunlight, and different parts of the Moon are lit as it moves through space.

A full Moon appears as a complete disc. As it slims to a crescent, it is called a waning Moon. As it grows full once more, it is said to be waxing. The small pictures opposite show the phases you can see.

▷ This map shows some of the main features of the Moon.

Craters
1 Plato
2 Aristarchus
3 Kepler
4 Copernicus
5 Ptolemaeus
6 Alphonsus
7 Arzachel
8 Schickard
9 Clavius

Maria ("seas")
10 Sea of Rains
11 Sea of Serenity
12 Sea of Tranquillity
13 Sea of Crises
14 Sea of Fertility
15 Southern Sea

Mountains
16 Apennines
17 Haemus
18 Leibnitz

▷ Phases of the Moon: crescent to full, then back to crescent again.

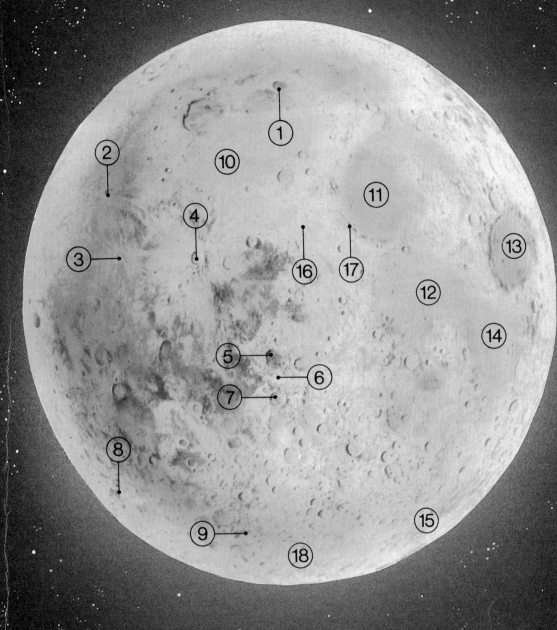

The nearest planets

△ This photograph of Mercury was taken by a Mariner spaceprobe. The planet is nearest to the Sun and its cratered surface is hot enough to boil lead.

The nearest planets to Earth are Mercury, Venus and Mars.

Mercury is about 36 million miles (58 million km) from the Sun. Because it stays close to the Sun in the sky, Mercury is difficult to see. Sometimes you can pick it out low in the western sky just after sunset, or low in the east just before sunrise.

Venus is much brighter than any other planet or star. It is the planet closest to Earth. Although Venus is bright, it is disappointing when viewed through a telescope, for the planet is covered with dense cloud. No details of its surface can be seen.

Mars is 142 million miles (228 million km) from the Sun. It appears as a reddish ball when viewed through a telescope. Unmanned spaceprobes have already landed on Mars, and manned spacecraft will probably go there in the future.

△ In 1976 two Viking
spacecraft landed on
Mars. They found that
the planet was a lifeless
desert covered in rocks
and sand.

▷ This picture shows
Venus, a planet about
the same size as Earth.
But unlike Earth, the air
of Venus is poisonous
and the heat greater
than an oven.

9

Gas giants

Jupiter is the largest planet in the Solar System. It contains more matter than the rest of the planets put together. Its atmosphere is deep and dense, and is made up mainly of hydrogen.

Swirling in the skies of Jupiter is an immense storm, the Great Red Spot. The Spot, which has been seen by astronomers for hundreds of years, must be the longest-lasting hurricane in the Solar System.

Beyond Jupiter is Saturn, the ringed planet. Saturn is much larger than Earth, and like Jupiter it has an atmosphere of hydrogen.

Saturn's rings are made of billions of tiny lumps of water-ice. Most range in size from a marble to a football, but a few may be as much as 6/10 mile (1 km) or more across. Although the rings themselves are about 170,500 miles (275,000 km) across, they are less than half a mile thick.

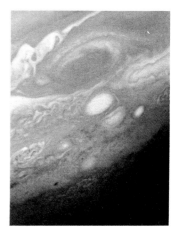

△ This photograph of Jupiter was taken by a *Voyager* spacecraft. It shows the Great Red Spot, which is big enough to swallow two planets the size of Earth with room to spare!

▷ This picture shows a *Voyager* cruising past Saturn. The photographs taken revealed hundreds of fine rings, banded like the grooves on an LP record. The small pictures show telescope views from Earth.

10

Frozen worlds

△ Pluto is 3.6 million miles (5.9 million km) from the Sun. At this distance the Sun appears no bigger than a very bright star, as this picture shows.

The three planets farthest from the Sun are Uranus, Neptune and Pluto. All are cold and forbidding.

Uranus was discovered in 1781 by the English astronomer William Herschel. The planet is so cold that even on its sunlit side, the temperature never climbs higher than −210°C. It has a system of thin, spidery rings.

We know very little about Neptune. No spacecraft has yet been there, and through a telescope we see only a tiny blue disc. It has two moons, Triton and Nereid, and an atmosphere of hydrogen and methane.

Compared to the other outer planets, Pluto is tiny — about the size of our own Moon. Pluto's orbit sometimes passes inside that of Neptune. Until 1999 Neptune, and not Pluto, will be the outermost planet. Pluto is thought to be made of gases such as methane and ammonia.

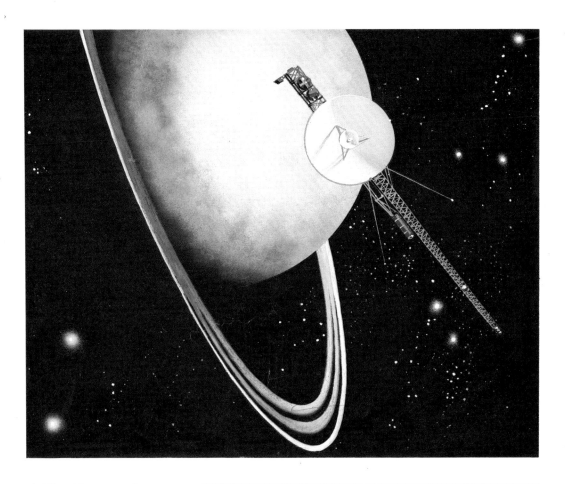

△ The *Voyager 2*
spaceprobe, launched in
1977, is expected to fly
by Uranus in January
1986. This picture shows
what the scene might be
like.

▷ *Voyager 2* is expected
to reach Neptune in
August 1989. In this view
the moon Triton can be
seen.

13

Stars of northern skies

△ Wear warm clothes when you go out at night. You will need a flashlight to look at the star charts in this book. A deckchair is good for comfy viewing.

When you first look at the night sky, it seems to be a jumbled mass of shining stars. The star map opposite and on page 17 will help you to pick out the main constellations. Constellations are groups of stars which form patterns or shapes in the sky.

One problem is that the constellations appear in different parts of the sky at different times of the year. Look for the clearest constellations first and use them as "pointers" to the other star groups. To use the star maps, turn the book until the present month is at the bottom. You should be able to see most of the stars in the middle and upper part of the star map.

The constellations

1	Andromeda	7	Cancer	14	Cetus
2	Aquarius	8	Canis Major	15	Columba
3	Aquila	9	Canis Minor	16	Corona Borealis
4	Aries	10	Capricornus	17	Corvus
5	Auriga	11	Cassiopeia	18	Cygnus
6	Bootes	12	Centaurus	19	Draco
		13	Cepheus	20	Eridanus

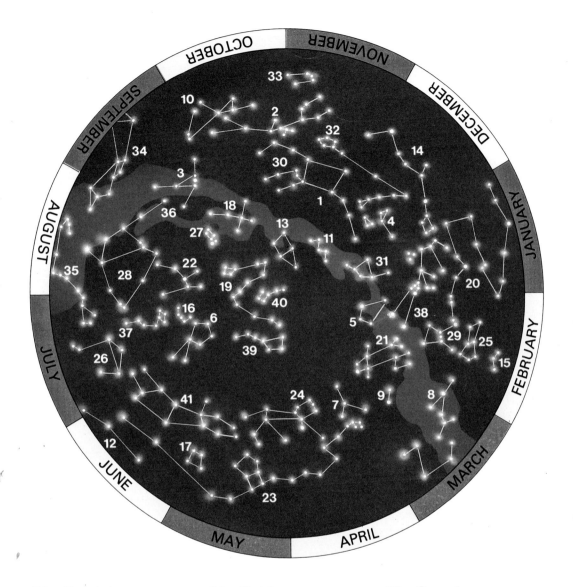

21	Gemini	28	Ophiucus	35	Scorpius
22	Hercules	29	Orion	36	Serpens Caput
23	Hydra	30	Pegasus	37	Serpens Cauda
24	Leo	31	Perseus	38	Taurus
25	Lepus	32	Pisces	39	Ursa Major
26	Libra	33	Pisces Austrinus	40	Ursa Minor
27	Lyra	34	Sagittarius	41	Virgo

Stars of southern skies

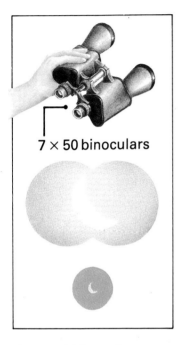

7 × 50 binoculars

△ 7 × 50 binoculars are just right for deckchair astronomy.

The map on the opposite page shows the constellations that can be seen in the southern half of the world. Crux, the Southern Cross, is the smallest but the easiest to spot.

The brightest star in the southern skies is Sirius in Canis Major. It can be found by following the angle of the three stars in the middle of Orion, the Hunter. These stars are known as Orion's "belt."

The Magellanic Clouds can also be seen. These are named after the explorer Ferdinand Magellan. They look like two misty patches, but are really satellite galaxies to the Milky Way.

The constellations
1 Ara
2 Aries
3 Aquarius
4 Aquila
5 Cancer
6 Canis Major
7 Canis Minor

8 Capricornus
9 Carina
10 Centaurus
11 Cetus
12 Corona Borealis
13 Corvus
14 Crater
15 Crux

16 Cygnus
17 Delphinus
18 Eridanus
19 Gemini
20 Grus
21 Hercules
22 Hydra
23 Leo

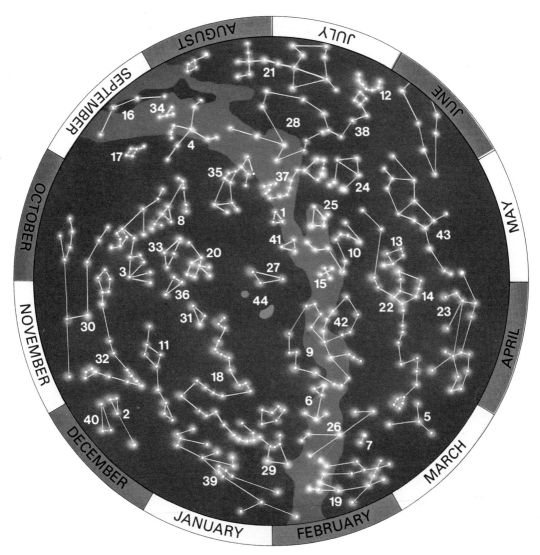

24	Libra	32	Pisces	40	Triangulum
25	Lupus	33	Pisces Austrinus	41	Triangulum
26	Monoceros	34	Sagitta		Australe
27	Octans	35	Sagittarius	42	Vela
28	Ophiucus	36	Sculptor	43	Virgo
29	Orion	37	Scorpius	44	Magellanic Clouds
30	Pegasus	38	Serpens		
31	Phoenix	39	Taurus		

* The pale blue band is the Milky Way.

17

Sky-watching

It soon becomes easy to find your way around the night sky. Once you know where to find some stars, you can use their position to find others.

▽ This sky map shows you the main stars and constellations in northern skies. Follow the arrows to find your way about the sky.

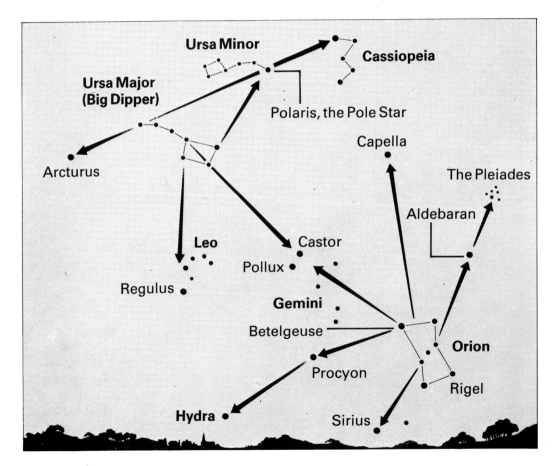

18

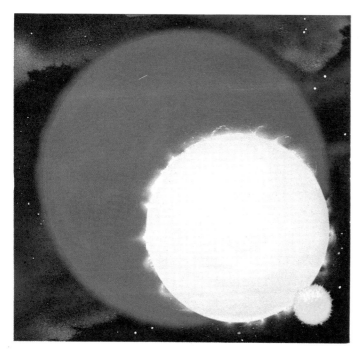

◁ Our Sun is small compared to many other stars. Here its size is matched against bright blue-white Rigel, and huge Aldebaran, which glows a dull red.

▽ Near Orion's "belt" is the Great Nebula. To the naked eye it looks like a hazy patch. Through a telescope, colourful clouds of dust and gas can be seen. Hydrogen glows red and white, while space dust appears blue.

More sky-watching

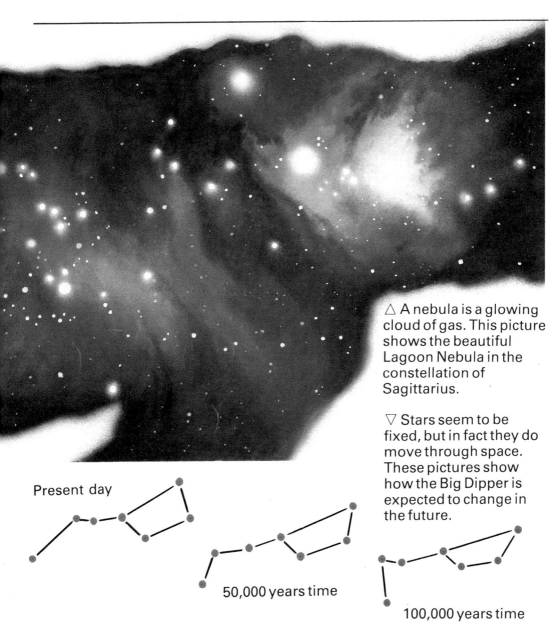

△ A nebula is a glowing cloud of gas. This picture shows the beautiful Lagoon Nebula in the constellation of Sagittarius.

▽ Stars seem to be fixed, but in fact they do move through space. These pictures show how the Big Dipper is expected to change in the future.

Present day

50,000 years time

100,000 years time

△ These are the
Pleiades, a group of
young stars in Taurus.
Seven stars can easily be
seen with the naked eye.
As many as 400 can be
seen through a
telescope.

▷ This is the
Andromeda galaxy. It is
the most distant object
that can be seen
with the
naked eye.

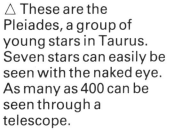

Galaxies

Our Solar System is only a small part of the Milky Way galaxy. The Sun is just one star in this swirl of 100 billion stars. On a clear night you can see it as a pale band, shining across the sky.

The Milky Way is one of millions of galaxies in the Universe. Galaxies are of three main types – spiral, elliptical and irregular – as shown on the right.

Because distances in space are so vast, astronomers have a special way of measuring distance. They measure in light years. This is the distance which light can travel in one year. As light travels at 186,000 miles (300,000 km) per second, one light year is 5.9 million million miles (9.5 million million km). The nearest star to the Solar System is Proxima Centauri, over 4 light years away. When you realize that the Milky Way is 100,000 light years across, you can begin to imagine the immense size of the Universe.

▷ This is how the Milky Way might look from far away in the depths of space.
▽ The three main types of galaxy.

Comets

△ Here you can see
Europe's *Giotto*
spaceprobe, which will
take photographs of
Halley's Comet.

Comets are rather like large dirty snowballs. Astronomers believe they are made of ice, rocks and dust.

Far out on the edge of the Solar System, a comet is a dark, frozen ball just a few miles across. Sometimes, though, a comet's orbit takes it close to the Sun. Then the surface layers of the comet boil away into space and form a huge glowing "tail," millions of miles long.

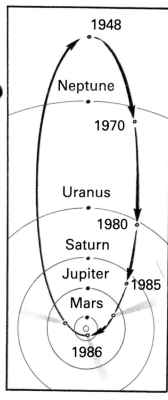

1948

Neptune

1970

Uranus

1980

Saturn

Jupiter

Mars

1985

1986

Halley's Comet is the most famous of them all. Astronomers have witnessed it for over 1,000 years. The comet was last seen in the skies in 1910. It comes close to the Sun about every 75 years or so, and it is due to return in 1986. This time, three spaceprobes (from Europe, Japan and Russia) and a giant space telescope (from the USA) will be in space to photograph and record its passing.

△ This plan shows the path of Halley's Comet on its way toward the Sun. After 1986 the comet will not be seen again until the year 2062.

Meteors

△ You need to stand outside for only a few minutes to spot a meteor flashing across the night sky. Meteors travel at high speeds, often up to 45 miles/second (72 km/second).

If you see a sudden streak of light falling across the night sky, it is probably a meteor. This is a piece of stone or iron that has entered the Earth's atmosphere from space.

Most meteors are very small, about the size of a grain of sand, and they burn up as they enter the atmosphere. The larger ones, varying in size from pebbles to boulders, do sometimes hit the ground.

While out in space, this piece of space debris is known as a meteoroid. If it burns up in the atmosphere, it is called a meteor. If it hits the ground, it is called a meteorite.

One of the largest known meteorites to hit Earth landed in the United States, in Arizona, in prehistoric times. This gigantic boulder was the size of a house and weighed 50,000 tons. It left a crater almost 1 mile (1.6 km) wide which can still be seen today.

△ The Moon was hit by millions of meteorites early in its history. The craters they made can still be seen today.

▷ Sometimes the Earth passes through a swarm of meteoroid particles. Then we get a "shower" of meteors which appear to come from the same point in space. This is called the "radiant." Here are the dates and radiants of important meteor showers.

Meteor showers to look for

Date	Name	Radiant
January 1–6	Quadrantids	Bootes
April 19–24	Lyrids	Lyra
May 1–8	Eta Aquarids	Aquarius
July 25–August 18	Perseids	Perseus
October 16–21	Orionids	Orion
October 20–November 30	Taurids	Taurus
December 7–15	Geminids	Gemini

Other sky sights

△ On the left you can see a solar eclipse. This happens when the Moon passes between the Sun and the Earth. The bright glow is the Sun's outer atmosphere, or corona.

On the right is a lunar eclipse. Here, the Moon passes into the shadow of the Earth and dims to a dull copper color.

When the Moon passes between the Sun and the Earth, it blots out most of the Sun's light. This is called a solar eclipse. At other times the Earth moves between the Sun and the Moon. This cuts off the Sun's light from the Moon, and the Moon fades to a dim copper tone. This is called a lunar eclipse.

Lunar eclipses happen less often than solar eclipses.

People living in or near the Arctic

Circle can often see the Northern Lights, or Aurora Borealis. These often appear as a glowing arc over the horizon. Sometimes rays of light stretch across the sky from this arc and form a gigantic moving "curtain" of many colours.

△ An aurora appears when electrical particles from the Sun are trapped in the Earth's upper atmosphere. This causes the atoms in the air to glow and form ghostly twisting "curtains" in the sky.

Lights like these are also seen in the southern half of the world, near the Antarctic. Here they are known as the Southern Lights, or Aurora Australis.

Glossary

Here is a list of some of the technical words in this book.

Aurora
A glowing "curtain" of light that appears near the North and South Poles of Earth. Jupiter also has them.

Asteroids
A belt of giant rocks, small planetoids and space debris. It moves between Mars and Jupiter.

Comet
A "dirty snowball" in space. It has a glowing tail when it nears the Sun.

Constellation
A group of stars which seem to form a pattern.

Corona
The outer layers of the Sun's atmosphere.

Eclipse
When one body passes into the shadow of another. A lunar eclipse happens when the shadow of the Earth falls on the Moon, cutting off the sunlight.

Galaxy
A group of millions of stars, often spiral in form. Our own galaxy is the Milky Way.

▽ These views are what you might expect to see through a good amateur telescope. The sizes of the planets vary as they move nearer or further from Earth in their orbits.

You can spot Jupiter's four biggest moons with any good pair of binoculars. Watch them moving across the sky from night to night.

Mercury

Venus

Mars

Jupiter

Saturn

Jupiter's moons

Light year
The distance light travels in one year. It is about 5.9 million million miles (9.5 million million km).

Meteor
A small piece of space rock or stone, flashing brightly as it burns up in the Earth's atmosphere. A piece which hits the Earth is called a meteorite.

Nebula
Cloud of gas and dust in space. Some contain stars and so shine. Others are dark.

Orbit
The path in which a small object repeatedly travels around a larger one. The Moon orbits the Earth once a month. The Earth orbits the Sun once a year.

Satellite
A small body, either natural or man-made, that orbits a planet. The Moon is Earth's natural satellite.

Star
A glowing ball of gas in space. The nearest star to Earth is the Sun.

Taking photographs

With care, you can take some interesting photographs of the night sky.

Any camera will do as long as it has a "B" setting. This allows you to take long time exposures to record the faint starlight on film.

Try using color film with a rating of 400 ASA, exposing for about 10 seconds. This will be enough to capture the brighter stars on film.

To get a picture like the one above, aim the camera at the Pole Star, (find out where it is on page 18). Support the camera firmly on a tripod or against a wall. Leave the shutter open for an hour or more. You should get these curving light images, as the Earth turns on its axis.

31

Index